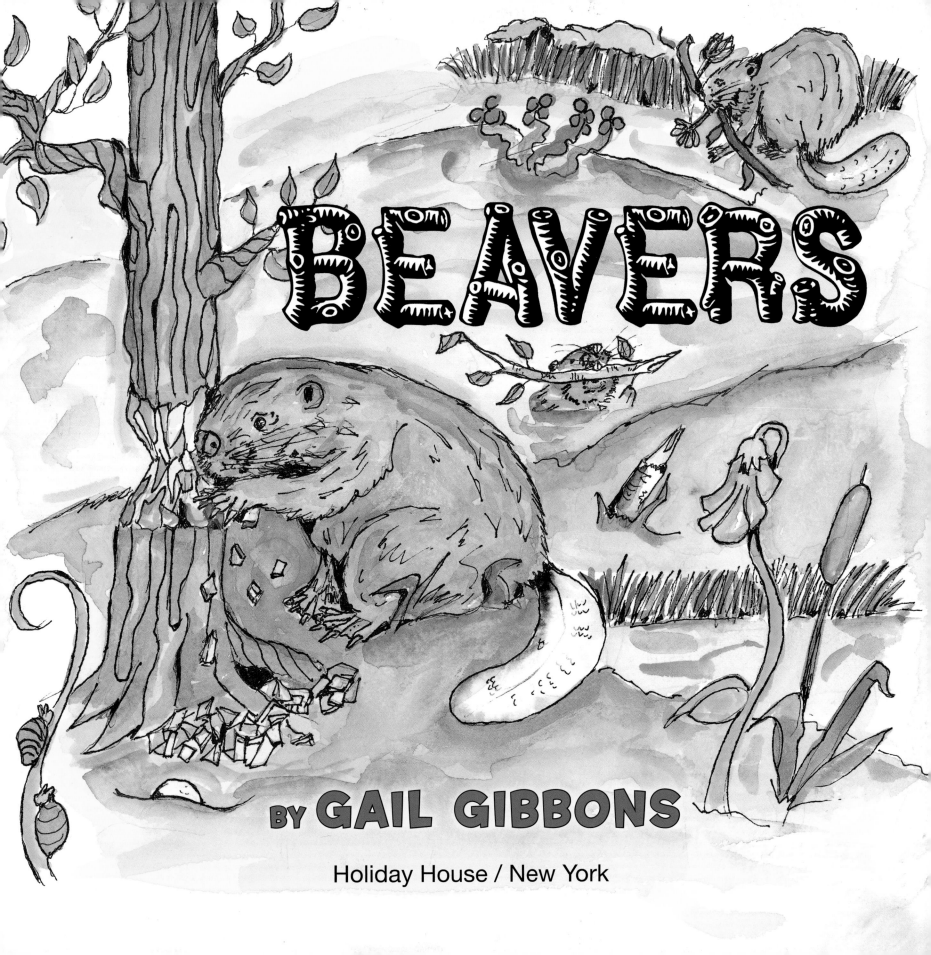

BEAVERS

BY GAIL GIBBONS

Holiday House / New York

To my husband, creative partner, and best friend, Kent

To Jim Doherty,
General Curator Emeritus of
the New York Zoological Society,
Bronx Zoo, New York

Printed and Bound in April 2013 at Toppan Leefung, DongGuan City, China.
www.holidayhouse.com
First Edition
1 3 5 7 9 10 8 6 4 2

Library of Congress Cataloging-in-Publication Data
Gibbons, Gail.
Beavers / by Gail Gibbons. — 1st ed.
p. cm.
ISBN 978-0-8234-2412-2 (hardcover)
1. Beavers—Juvenile literature. I. Title.
QL737.R632G527 2012
599.37—dc23
2011049420

Crunch . . . gnaw . . . CRASH! A beaver has used its strong front teeth to gnaw through the base of a tree.

The canal was dug by beavers to help float and move logs and other pieces of wood toward the damsite.

The beaver grasps one of the tree's branches and moves it down a canal toward the narrow part of a stream.

BUILDING A BEAVER DAM

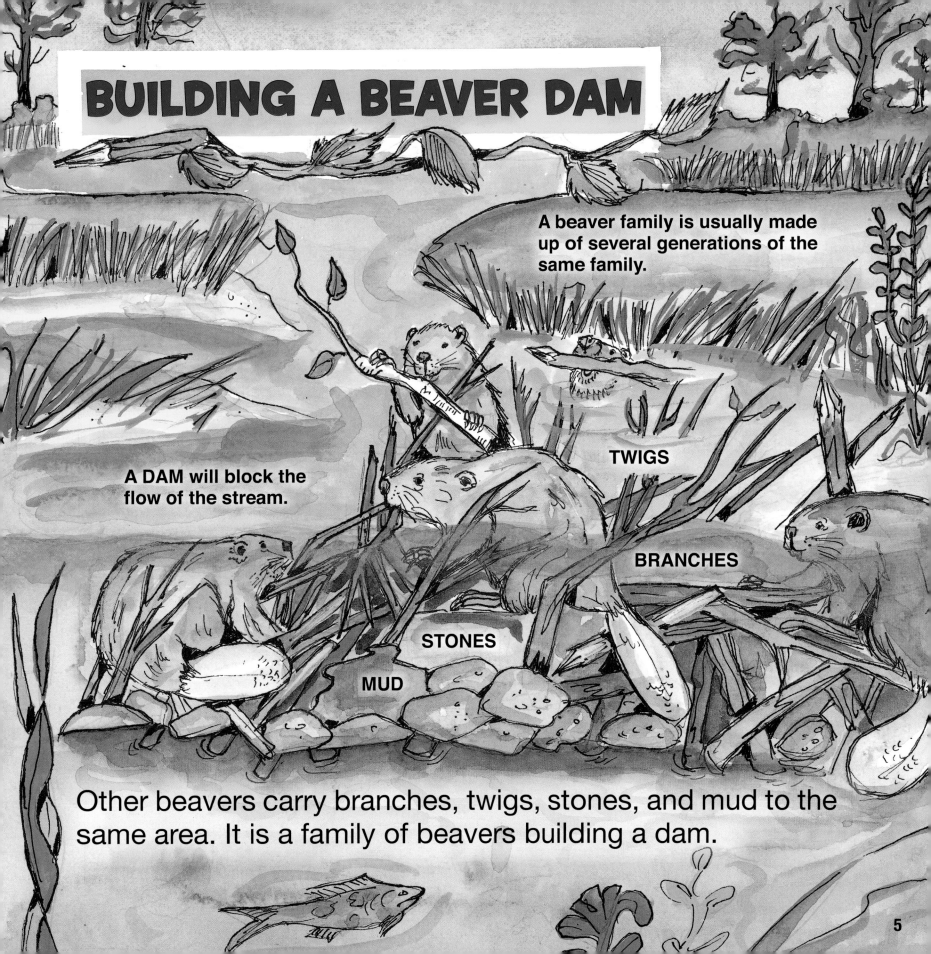

A beaver family is usually made up of several generations of the same family.

A DAM will block the flow of the stream.

TWIGS

BRANCHES

STONES

MUD

Other beavers carry branches, twigs, stones, and mud to the same area. It is a family of beavers building a dam.

More and more branches and twigs are shoved into the stream's muddy bottom. The dam gets taller as more logs, branches, and sticks are piled on top. Stones are put into place to hold the structure down. Mud is used to seal openings.

6

BEAVER POND

WATERLINE

The dam is built up to be higher than the waterline so water will back up to create a beaver pond. The beavers will be able to build their home in the pond.

BEAR

FOX

Beaver ponds are normally found in wetland areas with heavy forest vegetation.

The beaver pond has now become a good size. Beavers need trees and water to survive. They use trees for building, and they eat the bark and twigs of trees.

HAWK

WOLF

BOBCAT

OWL

WHERE BEAVERS LIVE

NORTH AMERICA

ATLANTIC OCEAN

EUROPE

ASIA

PACIFIC OCEAN

AFRICA

EQUATOR

SOUTH AMERICA

INDIAN OCEAN

AUSTRALIA

The EQUATOR is an imaginary line around the middle of Earth, equally distant from the North Pole and the South Pole.

ANTARCTICA

Living in and around water protects beavers from enemies. If danger comes near, the beavers can usually dive and swim away.

BUILDING A BEAVER LODGE

BASE OF LODGE

The larger beavers are able to move 30-to-40-pound (13.6-to-18-kilogram) stones into place.

A beaver home is called a lodge. Beavers begin to build their lodge by piling up stones, sticks, small logs, and mud underwater.

LODGE FLOOR

The beavers go back and forth lugging, pushing, and stacking more and more building material. An island begins to appear. Soon they have built the lodge floor, with enough room for the entire family of beavers.

Stones are put into place to secure logs, branches, and other things.

The beavers use their tails and their front feet to pat mud around the structure to hold it together. As the mud hardens, the lodge becomes waterproof.

Next the beavers arrange branches and stones above the lodge floor. It is the beginning of a dome-shaped structure. Back and forth, again and again, they add more branches, stones, and mud.

In case they need to escape, beavers dig PLUNGE HOLES not far from the water's edge.

PLUNGE HOLES

AIR VENT at top

ROOF

It takes about one week for a family of beavers to build a lodge. The family is always fixing it up and doing repairs.

WALLS

An average lodge is about 5 to 8 feet (1.5 to 2.4 meters) above the waterline and is about 10 to 13 feet (3 to 4 meters) in diameter.

TUNNEL

The beavers gnaw and dig tunnels from the underwater base of the lodge up to the lodge floor so they can come and go. Finally, the beavers smooth the lodge floor with mud. They cover it with soft, dry leaves and other plants to make the floor soft and dry.

A BEAVER'S BODY

OUTER GUARD FUR keeps the beaver dry.

INNER SOFT FUR keeps the beaver warm.

BACK

FUR COLOR blends in with surroundings.

TAIL is thick, broad, scaly, and flat. On land, a beaver moves awkwardly and uses its tail for balance.

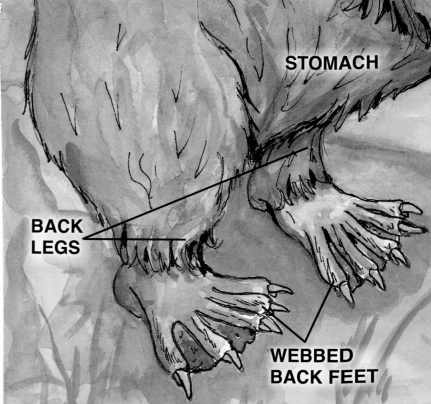

STOMACH

BACK LEGS

WEBBED BACK FEET

A BEAVER'S BACK FEET

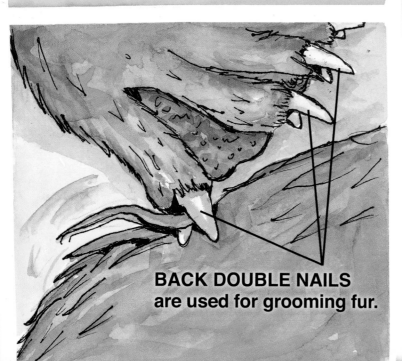

BACK DOUBLE NAILS are used for grooming fur.

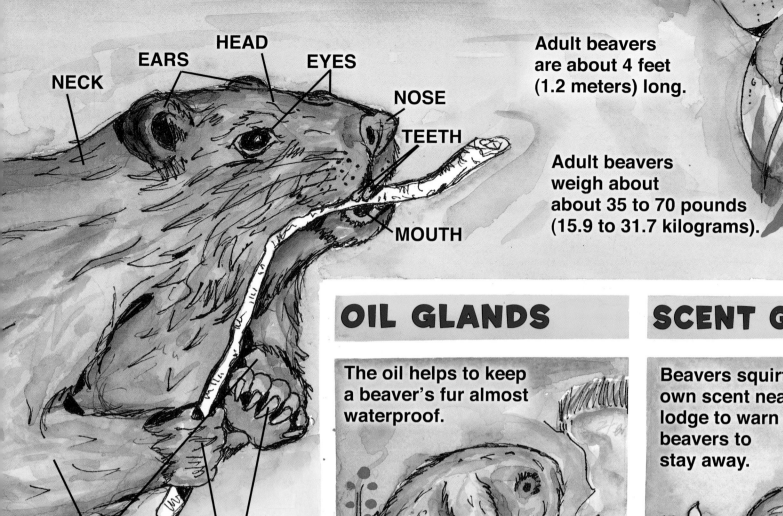

NECK

EARS

HEAD

EYES

NOSE

TEETH

MOUTH

FRONT LEGS

FRONT FEET and FRONT NAILS are used for holding, carrying, and digging.

Adult beavers are about 4 feet (1.2 meters) long.

Adult beavers weigh about about 35 to 70 pounds (15.9 to 31.7 kilograms).

OIL GLANDS

The oil helps to keep a beaver's fur almost waterproof.

SCENT GLANDS

Beavers squirt their own scent near the lodge to warn other beavers to stay away.

A beaver has two sets of glands under its tail. The first set of glands contains oil that the beaver spreads over its fur while grooming. The second set of glands contains sweet-smelling oil used to "mark" its territory.

15

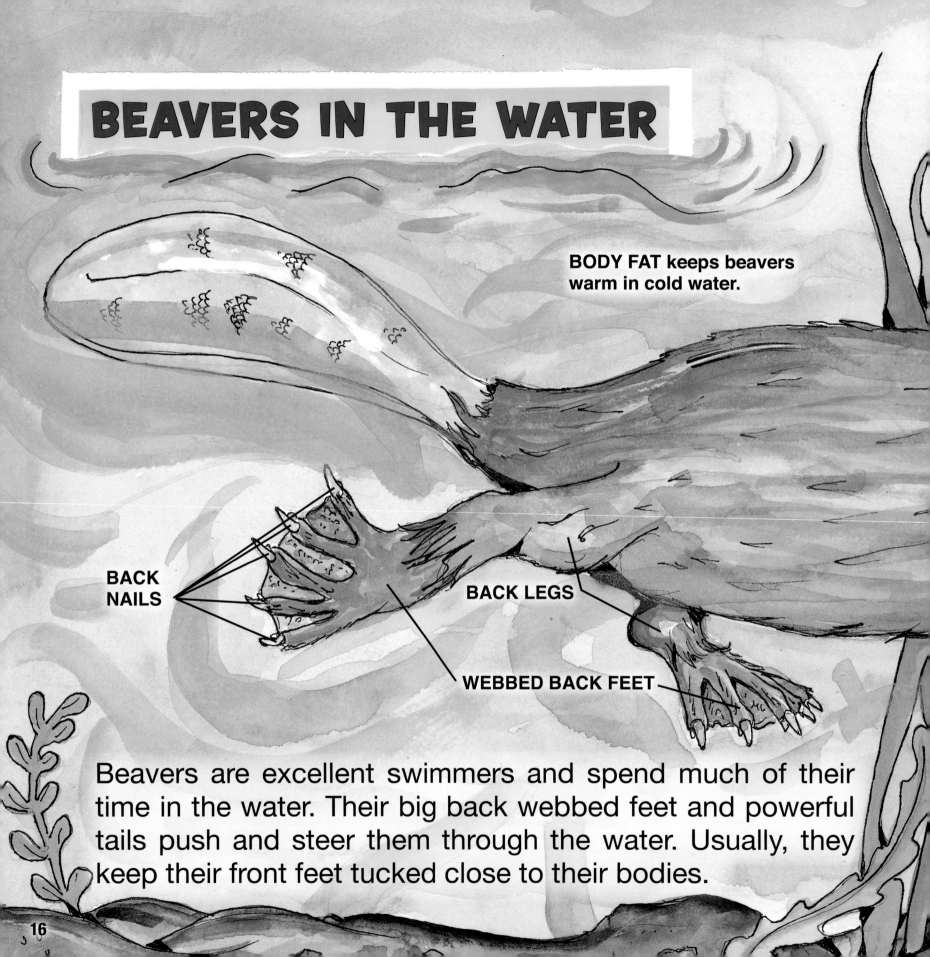

BEAVERS IN THE WATER

BODY FAT keeps beavers warm in cold water.

BACK NAILS

BACK LEGS

WEBBED BACK FEET

Beavers are excellent swimmers and spend much of their time in the water. Their big back webbed feet and powerful tails push and steer them through the water. Usually, they keep their front feet tucked close to their bodies.

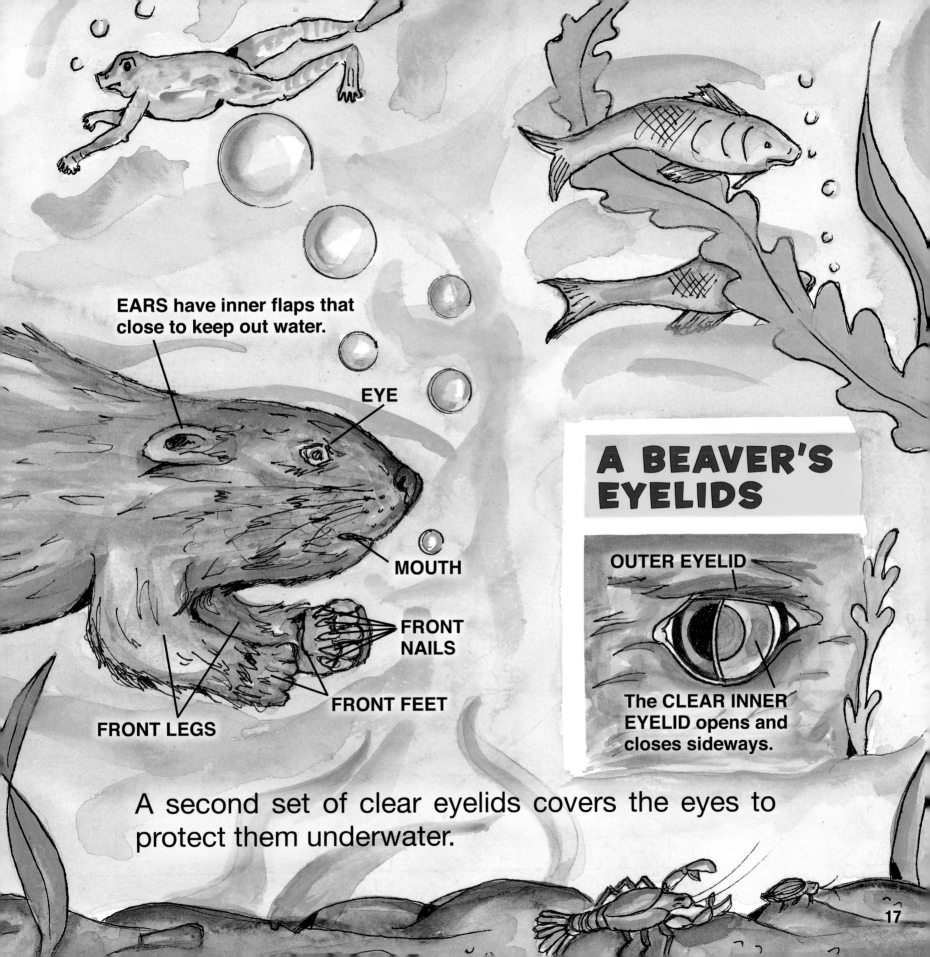

EARS have inner flaps that close to keep out water.

EYE

MOUTH

FRONT NAILS

FRONT FEET

FRONT LEGS

A BEAVER'S EYELIDS

OUTER EYELID

The CLEAR INNER EYELID opens and closes sideways.

A second set of clear eyelids covers the eyes to protect them underwater.

WHAT BEAVERS EAT

CATTAILS

Favorite trees are ASPENS, WILLOWS, BIRCHES, and POPLARS.

Beavers have very strong STOMACH ACID and long intestines to help digest their woody diet.

NUTS

BERRIES

BUDS

SEEDS

Beavers are plant eaters, also called herbivores. They eat bark, twigs, and roots of trees. They also eat berries, cattails, seeds, nuts, buds, and other plant life.

THE JAWS AND TEETH OF A BEAVER

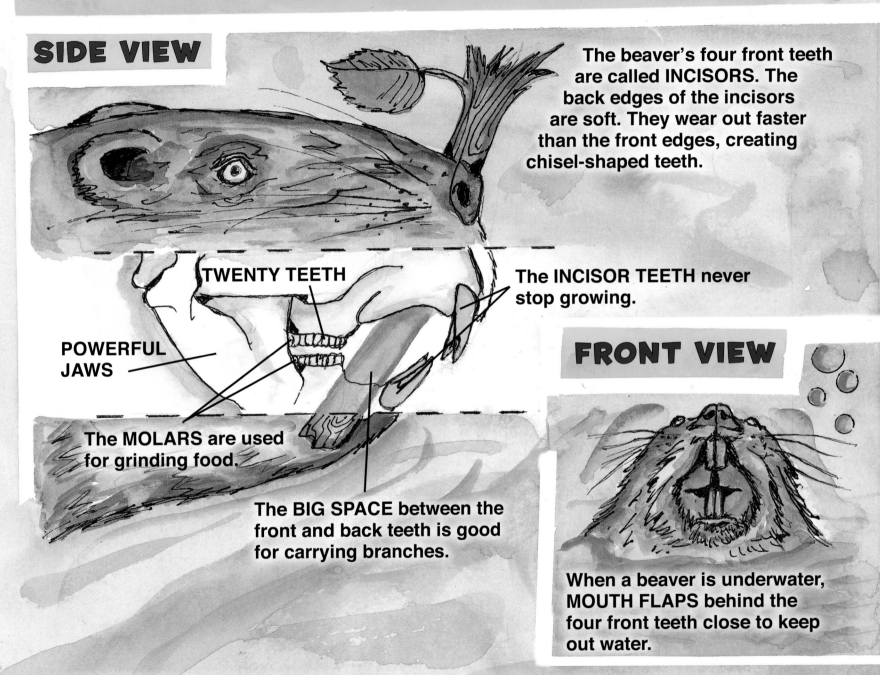

SIDE VIEW

The beaver's four front teeth are called INCISORS. The back edges of the incisors are soft. They wear out faster than the front edges, creating chisel-shaped teeth.

TWENTY TEETH

POWERFUL JAWS

The INCISOR TEETH never stop growing.

The MOLARS are used for grinding food.

The BIG SPACE between the front and back teeth is good for carrying branches.

FRONT VIEW

When a beaver is underwater, MOUTH FLAPS behind the four front teeth close to keep out water.

A beaver needs powerful jaws and sharp front teeth to gnaw away at trees constantly.

COMMUNICATION

EARS

EYES

NOSE

Beavers make many vocal sounds, almost always chattering aloud. Whining and whimpering sounds often mean they want something or are scared. They warn other beavers or enemies by whistling, hissing, or growling. Beavers show affection or greet other beavers by nibbling the other beavers' cheeks.

DANGER! If a beaver senses an enemy nearby . . . *WHACK!* It slaps its tail on the water's surface, making a very loud, snapping sound. Other beavers go on alert. They hurry back to the lodge.

A beaver can't see very well. It does have a very good sense of hearing, even for faraway sounds. A beaver's most important sense is its sense of smell. It can find family members, locate food, and smell to detect enemies.

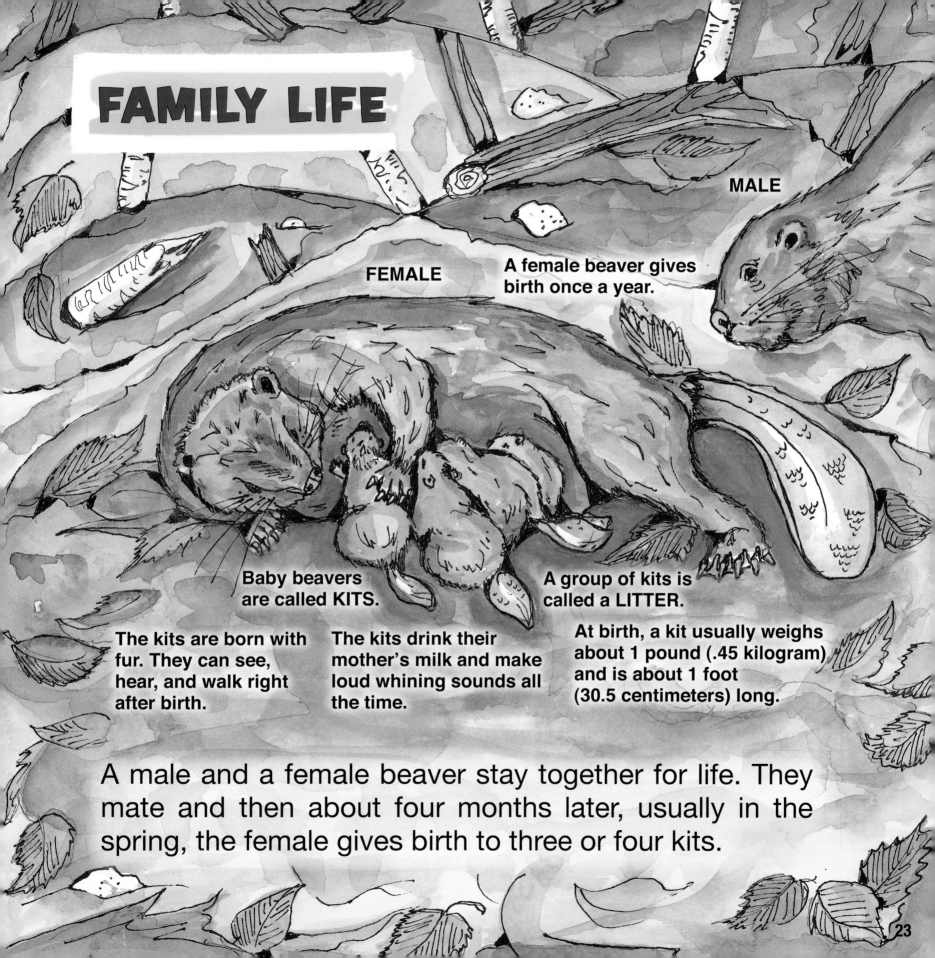

FAMILY LIFE

MALE

FEMALE

A female beaver gives birth once a year.

Baby beavers are called KITS.

A group of kits is called a LITTER.

The kits are born with fur. They can see, hear, and walk right after birth.

The kits drink their mother's milk and make loud whining sounds all the time.

At birth, a kit usually weighs about 1 pound (.45 kilogram) and is about 1 foot (30.5 centimeters) long.

A male and a female beaver stay together for life. They mate and then about four months later, usually in the spring, the female gives birth to three or four kits.

23

The kits play and chase one another. This helps them build strong muscles.

At about three months old, the kits leave the lodge with their parents. The kits are learning skills needed for survival.

In a few weeks, the kits begin swimming inside the tunnels where it is safe. At about two months of age, the parents begin bringing solid food to the kits so they can learn to nibble, gnaw, and chew.

At one year old, a beaver weighs about 25 pounds (11.3 kilograms).

At about two years old, the young beavers will be able to go out on their own. Sometimes they build a lodge of their own in the same pond.

When the young beavers are about one year old, they have learned enough and are strong enough to help their family. They cut down trees. They help repair any damage done to their lodge and dam. They stay alert to danger.

If ice forms on the water, the beavers can swim through the tunnels to their stash of food.

In the fall beavers actively begin storing their food in a pile underwater away from their lodge. This helps to keep the woody plants fresh and soft during the winter.

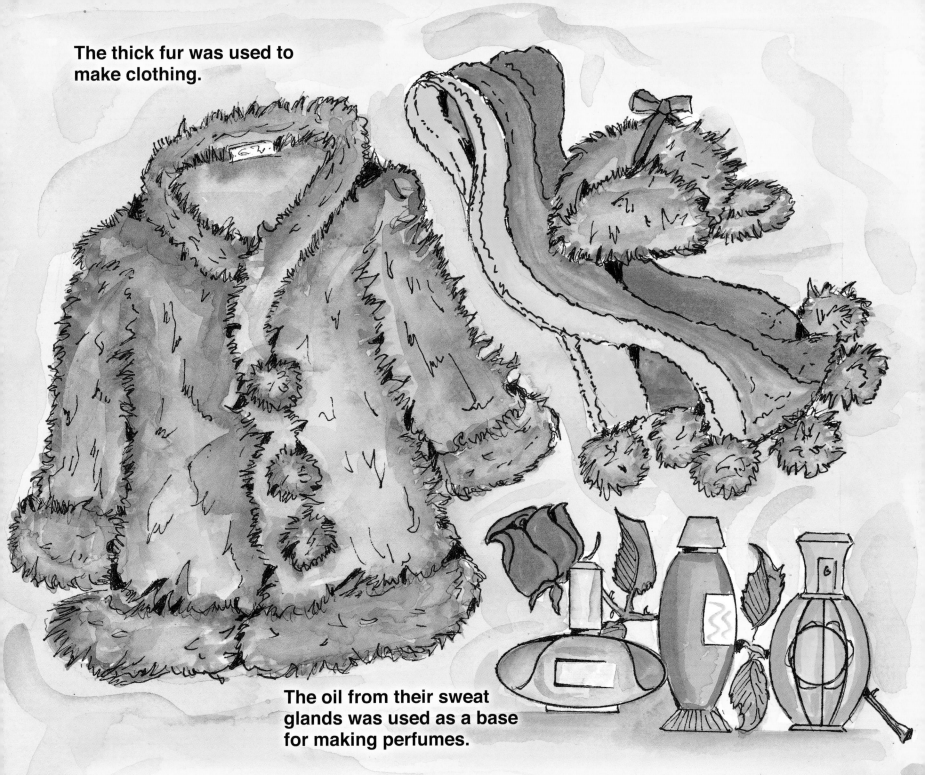

The thick fur was used to make clothing.

The oil from their sweat glands was used as a base for making perfumes.

Beavers have enemies. Their greatest enemies are humans. Beavers have been hunted for many years for their beautiful fur and their sweet-smelling scent oil.

Where wetlands have been filled in to create land sites for building, beaver populations have declined.

The pond provides water, food, and a safe place for other animals.

Today people realize how important beavers are in the balance of nature. From their building skills new wetlands are formed. Older wetlands may fill in with rich earth and become meadows. The wildlife living in the wetlands and meadows benefit. In other areas beaver dams help control flooding during heavy rains by holding back the rising water.

In many places wetland preserves have been created. People often visit them hoping to see beavers and the other wildlife living in their natural environment. There, beaver populations are on the rise.

People are lucky if they get to see a beaver or
a group of beavers busily at work.

BEAVERS...BEAVERS...BEAVERS...

Beavers are members of the rodent family, all of which have four front teeth that never stop growing. Some of the beaver's relatives are mice, rats, and squirrels.

Beavers are nocturnal, meaning they are most active at night. They are easiest to spot in the early morning and early evening.

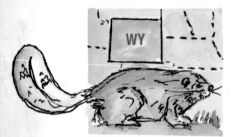

The largest beaver ever found weighed 115 pounds (52.2 kilograms). It was found in Wyoming in 1938.

A beaver never stops growing, but it slows down as it ages.

Beavers usually live to be about twelve years old.

A beaver usually stays underwater from three to five minutes. If necessary it can stay underwater for about fifteen minutes.

A beaver can swim 5 miles (8 kilometers) an hour.

The world's largest known beaver dam is located in northwestern Canada. It measures about 2,788 feet (849.8 meters) long. It is believed to be about forty years old.

WEBSITES:
www.beaversww.org
www.thecanadianencyclopedia.
beavers.com